Journey Through the Church Year

The Time
of the
Church

Written by Suzanne Richterkessing • Illustrated by Susan Morris

4321 N. Ballard Road, Appleton, WI 54919-0001
www.aal.org • e-mail: aalmail@aal.org • (800) 225-5225

© 1999 Aid Association for Lutherans

Published by Concordia Publishing House
3558 S. Jefferson Avenue, St. Louis, MO 63118-3968
Manufactured in the United States of America

2   3   4   5   6   7   8   9   10   08   07   06   05   04   03   02   01   00   99

The church library was quiet except for the ticking of the clock on the wall.

"Smudge! Smudge! Where are you?"

Smudge looked up from the book he was reading. "There you are!" said Smidge. "I'm glad that Elder Mouse taught us how to read. It's time to learn more from him. Let's go to class, just like the children we see on Sundays."

Smidge and Smudge reached their classroom just as Elder Mouse was checking his watch. "You made it with only a whisker to spare," he said with a chuckle.

"Smudge, please read the word on the chalkboard," Elder Mouse directed, pointing to the broken piece of chalkboard he had found in a Sunday school trash can.

"Pen … te … cost," Smudge said slowly as he sounded out the word.

"That's right! Pentecost!" repeated Elder Mouse. "Sunday is Pentecost, indeed, indeed."

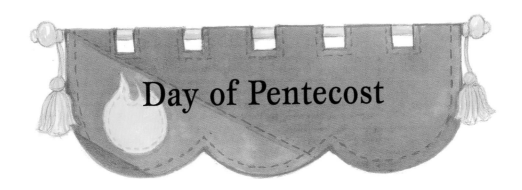

Day of Pentecost

"Pentecost is exactly 50 days after Easter Sunday," Elder Mouse said. "God's people will hear the Bible story of how Jesus' friends gathered together for prayer. Suddenly, there was a noise like a rushing wind, and flames of fire appeared above their heads. They began to speak in languages they did not know before. The Holy Spirit had come to each of Jesus' friends. God was with them in a new way. They began to tell others the wonderful news that Jesus had lived and died for them."

Smudge listened carefully. As soon as class was over, he dashed back to the library, leaving Smidge behind. He had work to do!

"Peh … peh … Pentecost," Smudge said to himself as he thumbed through the pages of a book. He began to read out loud.

"Pentecost is a festival day. The Holy Spirit came on the first Pentecost as flames of fire. The color of the altar cloth is red to remind the congregation that the Holy Spirit creates faith in their hearts.

"The Holy Spirit gave Jesus' friends words to say that helped them tell others about God's love and His plan for them. The Day of Pentecost is like the birthday of the church."

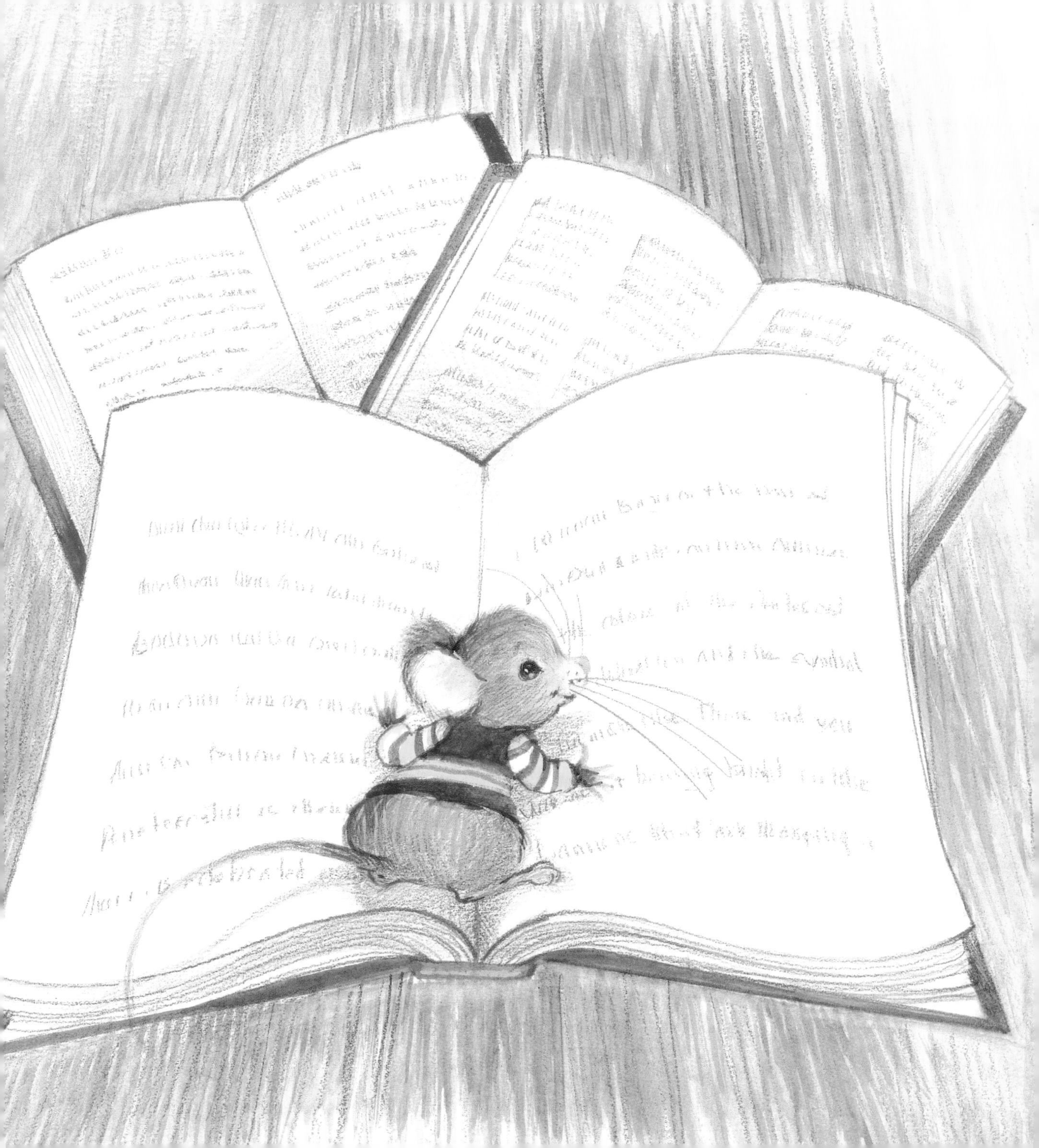

Smudge had an idea. He found a piece of paper and placed it on the table next to the book. Then he scampered to a Sunday school room and carefully selected some crayons.

Back in the library, he began to draw. He worked slowly using red, yellow and orange crayons. He printed the words "Day of Pentecost" at the top of the page.

Smudge carefully rolled up the piece of paper. Clutching it tightly, he returned to the old briefcase. There was no sign of Smidge, so Smudge hung the picture where she would certainly see it.

As Smidge entered, Smudge covered her eyes. "I have a present for you!" he announced. "Ta-da!" Smudge removed his paws from Smidge's eyes.

"Oh, Smudge," exclaimed Smidge. "What a good reminder of Pentecost."

Smidge had an idea. She had been watching the church quilters. Using teeny tiny stitches, she worked late into the night to make a perfect copy of Smudge's flame. She showed her project to Smudge the next day.

"Elder Mouse has taught us many things about living in the church," Smidge said. "Let's make a gift to say thank you. You can draw the symbols of the church year, and I will sew copies to give to Elder Mouse."

Smudge's eyes sparkled as he said, "That's a splendid idea. Indeed, indeed!"

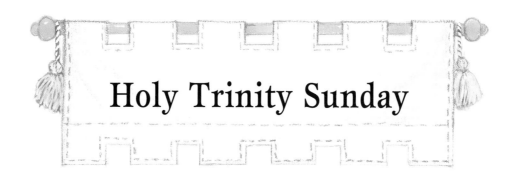

Holy Trinity Sunday

Elder Mouse decided to take a short vacation. As he said goodbye, he gave Smidge and Smudge an assignment. "I want you to learn more about the next festival. It's about the great Three in One," he said.

Because that was the only clue Elder Mouse gave, Smudge worked all week to discover the name of the festival. He held up his paper as he explained what he had learned to Smidge. He had drawn a triangle. Each of the three sides was the same length.

"People use the name Trinity to describe God the Father, who made all things, God the Son, who died to save all people, and God the Holy Spirit, who helps people believe," Smudge told Smidge.

"One side of the triangle is for God the Father. One side is for Jesus, the Son of God. And one side is for the Holy Spirit," Smudge continued. "There are three sides but only one triangle, just like there are three Persons in the Trinity but only one God."

"Three in One!" Smidge added as she carefully sewed a triangle on a piece of white cloth.

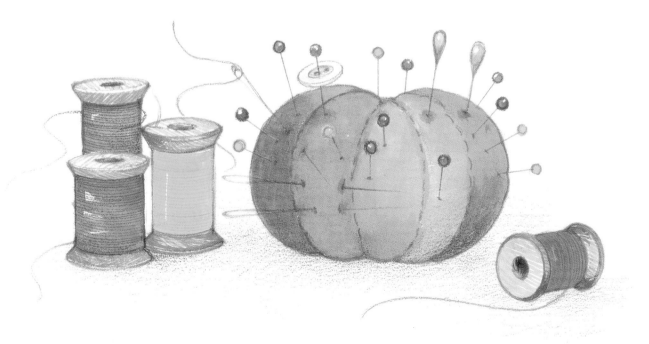

Season After Pentecost

When Elder Mouse returned from his trip, he congratulated the young mice on their research. Then he told them that the days after Pentecost make up the longest season in the church year. This season lasts from late spring, all through summer and into fall.

"During the days after Pentecost, God's people are reminded that the Holy Spirit helps them share Jesus' love with others," Elder Mouse said.

Smudge drew a dove as the symbol for the Holy Spirit. Smidge sewed a dove on green cloth that was exactly the same color that was on the altar. The color green reminded her that the Holy Spirit helps the faith of God's people grow.

During the hot summer and into the cool fall, Smidge and Smudge remembered all of the festivals and celebrations they had learned about. Smudge made so many drawings that they filled the briefcase.

In her teeny tiny stitches, Smidge copied all of the symbols onto fabric and placed them in a secret box.

Elder Mouse continued teaching the young mice. He smiled as he thought to himself that Smidge and Smudge were very bright little mice. Indeed, indeed!

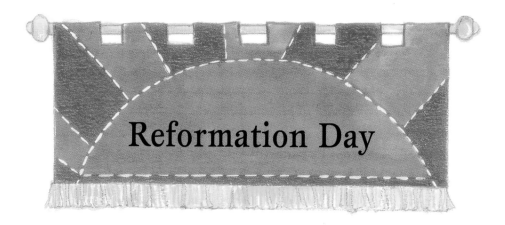

Reformation Day

As the days after Pentecost neared an end, Smidge and Smudge were eager for a change. They knew something was about to happen when the colors on the altar changed from green to red. The color red meant it was a special day.

"Something's happening!" they exclaimed together. They ran to find Elder Mouse and learn about this celebration.

Elder Mouse sat down, cleared his throat, and began to teach. "Right you are, Smidge and Smudge! The people will celebrate the Festival of the Reformation. October 31 is called Reformation Day because the people remember the work of a man named Martin Luther. He taught the church that God's gift of heaven is free to everyone who believes in Jesus! Indeed, indeed."

Smudge dashed to the library to find a book about Martin Luther and the Reformation. He learned that Martin Luther wrote the hymn "A Mighty Fortress Is Our God," which says God is like a strong castle in which His people are protected.

Smudge found a symbol, carefully copied it and took the drawing to Smidge. "This is called Luther's seal," he said. "Hey, I just thought of something. We are in a 'Lutheran' church. I'll bet it is named after Martin Luther!" Smudge announced.

Smidge smiled and began to sew a cloth picture of Luther's seal.

Christ the King Sunday

"I didn't know so much happened in a church year," Smudge said as he helped Smidge stuff the squares of fabric into the box. "I can't wait to give our present to Elder Mouse."

But Smidge and Smudge did have to wait. They discovered there was one more special day of the church year. Christ the King Sunday would happen near the end of November.

"Christ the King Sunday is sometimes called the Sunday of the Fulfillment," Smudge read from a book he had found. "God's people are reminded that Jesus will come again, and all believers will live with Him in heaven." Smudge drew a crown as the symbol for Smidge to copy as she sewed.

After the church service on Christ the King Sunday, Smidge and Smudge raced home to get their gift for Elder Mouse. Their excited chatter stopped when they discovered the box with all the fabric squares was gone!

Smidge and Smudge searched everywhere in the church for the box. As they got closer to the entrance, they heard Elder Mouse gasping, "My, oh my! Indeed, indeed, indeed, indeed!"

Smidge and Smudge skidded to a stop next to Elder Mouse. He was staring at a beautiful cloth banner. Someone had found the box and sewn some of the fabric squares together.

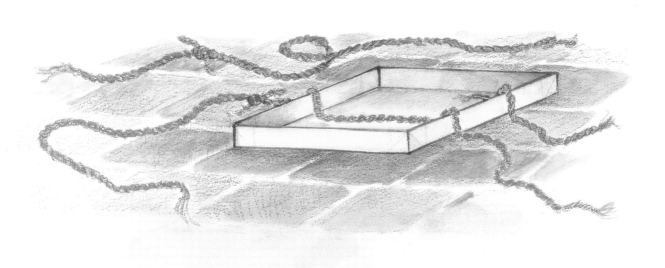

The square on the bottom of the banner read, "For Elder Mouse, a great teacher. Indeed, indeed!"

Elder Mouse looked at Smidge and Smudge and said, "I'm proud of you. You have learned well and you have made an important contribution. Now you are real church mice, ready to start the church year all over again!"

GOD'S
PEOPLE
WORSHIP
THROUGH THE
CHURCH
YEAR

For Elder Mouse,
a great teacher.
Indeed, indeed!